When Living Was a Labor Camp

Camino del Sol

A Latina and Latino Literary Series

When Living Was a Labor Camp

Diana García

THE UNIVERSITY OF ARIZONA PRESS

TUCSON

The University of Arizona Press
© 2000 Diana García

Library of Congress Cataloging-in-Publication Data
García, Diana, 1950–
When living was a labor camp / Diana García.
p. cm. — (Camino del sol)
ISBN 0-8165-2043-7 (pbk.: alk. paper)
1. Mexican Americans—Poetry. 2. Mexican American women—Poetry.
3. Children of migrant laborers—Poetry. I. Title. II. Series.
PS3557.A664 W48   2000   99-050792
811'.6—DC21

Publication of this book is made possible in part by the proceeds of a
permanent endowment created with the assistance of a Challenge Grant
from the National Endowment for the Humanities, a federal agency.

Manufactured in the United States of America on
acid-free, archival-quality paper.

12   11   10   8   7   6   5   4

For my parents, con amor
For Mike, mi corazón

Contents

Camp Observations

☙

My poems begin at five in the morning, any weekday morning between February and November in the middle of California's San Joaquín Valley. The old plastic-cased radio sputters. Two rooms away, I hear that snapcracklepop. We're on! All of us, every single set of ears in that house, pretend not to hear the sweep of violin, the throaty brass, the twelve-stringed guitars, the anonymous announcer crying *KXAX, Radio Campesino.* The opening to "La verdolaga" takes hold; we begin again.

Outside, if it's winter, tule fog blankets sky and ground. If it's summer, we'll be sizzling in ninety-degree weather by 10 A.M. Inside, the radio sings, the coffee pot clatters, eggs sputter in a cast iron skillet. Practical sounds: the clump of work boots on the kitchen linoleum. Mexican sounds: *¿Quieres papas? ¿Vas a querer un plátano en tu lonche?*

Those of us not going out to the fields or out to the construction site slide down deeper in bed. We know we're next. We know the bacon and egg routine. If we say we're not hungry, we'll get stewed prunes. No problem: we eat the bacon and eggs.

When I write about the morning routine years later, I understand I gotta be able to fill in where needed. I fill in with poems about the lives of people I knew in the San Joaquín Valley, about lives like those of the people I know. Most of those people migrated from Durango and Chihuahua, from Arizona and the Imperial Valley. Others migrated from Louisiana and Oklahoma, China, France, and Italy.

A man—I don't know his name; I've never met him—came to California in the 1930s, a dust bowl fugitive. He lived in one of the labor camps I write about, Camp Montgomery, not Camp CPC where my parents lived when I was born. Camp Montgomery is still there, some of the cabins. The fig orchard disappeared in the late 1990s. The last time I drove past, fig trees were piled as if to build a funeral pyre. Their twisted trunks and gnarled branches reminded me of the old people from the camps, too old and arthritic to work in the fields, waiting in an old Windsor chair by the front door.

Anyway, that Oklahoma fugitive read a copy of my poem, "When living was a labor camp called Montgomery," that my mother had given his daughter. He remembered Montgomery. He probably didn't know who Miguel Aceves Mejía was, my parents' favorite singer. The old man never cared much (I could have written: never gave a fig) for mariachi music. But he remembered the camp. He knew thick summer days sorting boxes of dried figs. He knew the sticky fig honey on his hands and face, knew flies sticking to him like flypaper.

What he and the people from the camps shared were years of hard hot days, cold foggy nights. Dreams of buying a house someday. A house with a thick foundation. A house with a few good lines. You could remodel this house, enclose its California bungalow porch with smoked picture windows, replace the double-hung windows with sliding aluminum, tinker with the kitchen and the bath. I know lives like this.

I write what I hear and see, the stories my dad, his friends and brothers, my godfather tell over six-packs of beer and plates piled with tacos. I listen to the aunts gossip in the kitchen, voices hushed as they recall some long-ago tragedy. The men howl at how they almost got swept up by la migra. The women weep for husbands killed by pesticides, nephews and nieces killed in a fire when the kerosene heater exploded. And always the guitars and songs, one uncle's clear baritone, my father's perfect harmony, the women listening for tones long forgotten.

I write what I eat and smell. Roasted jalapeños mixed with tomatoes canned last summer. Fresh flour tortillas rolled around chunks of roast beef. Refried beans oozing lard and jack cheese. Salsa, beef, cheese. The scent of Coty face powder and Emeraude cologne against a layer of Dixie Peach pomade. Peaches rotting beneath a mound of flies, the dry dust of the orchards in August.

The old orchards and fields are disappearing. New houses multiply where fig trees once grew. Former pasture land stands ready to nurture the newest University of California.

I know children in San Diego's North County who'd love to live in a camp like Montgomery or CPC. Instead they climb out of canyons beneath some of the most exclusive neighborhoods in the county. Their parents walk them to the strawberry and flower fields where the parents work. They bathe their children's hands and faces in irrigation water. They send them to school an hour before the first bus comes to pick them up.

In the 1930s, we suffered a depression. The U.S. government responded with the Repatriation Act: thousands of Mexican migrant workers were shipped back home. At the California–Arizona border, posted guards even turned back dust bowl migrants. Thankfully, both efforts were like sweeping back the tide. Years later, in the early 1950s, the Second World War and Korea behind us, returned veterans demanded education and better homes. They shouted slogans like *America for Americans*. The U.S. government responded with Operation Wetback: send wetbacks back where they came from. This sentiment spreads like thick tule fog today. Ask the former San Diego mayor who commandeers the Light Up the Border forces at the San Diego–Tijuana border on irregular Friday nights. Ask the backers of Propositions 187 and 227 in California. Ask the former mayor of National City, California, who declared, "Those Cubans are the worst kind of Mexicans there are."

An early mentor instructed me to write what I know. The title poem for this collection, "When living was a labor camp called Montgomery," came to me one summer afternoon while listening to my mother, her cousins and all their husbands laugh about their teenage days in Montgomery. The occasion was a festive one: no funeral to attend. We were celebrating another aunt's and uncle's fiftieth wedding anniversary. Their voices and stories stayed with me in the weeks and months that followed. I heard their voices while teaching poetry workshops to children whose first language was Tarasco and Zapotec. These were children for whom Spanish was a second language, English a third. They could have been children of the camps if they had had camps to call home. The first two sections of this collection, "An Orchard of Figs in the Fall" and "When Living Was a Labor Camp Called Montgomery," give voice to all those experiences.

The poems contained in "Serpentine Voices" and "Breasting the Rogue" are in response to Helene Cixous's exhortation to "write the body." They're also a reaction to marianismo, a devotion to the Virgin Mary that precludes any untoward behavior on the part of women, including women characters in fiction and poetry. For my models I call on María Luisa Bombal, Carmen Boullosa, Angeles Mastretta, Luisa Valenzuela, and Elena Poniatowska. I call on Sandra Cisneros, Ana Castillo, Pat Mora, and Denise Chávez. Their poems, novels, and short stories inspired me to write the lives of women who made their way out of the camps, women whose histories left them ill-suited to succeed in the cities. You can't be too nice or too proper to succeed in the city, no husband, no education, no job experience. Just a couple of kids and a car that needs a new gasket.

As a child, I was my maternal grandmother's changuita, her pobrecita, the poor monkey she pitied because I could never be beautiful. I was so dark. Perhaps that's why I was one of her favorites. In my mid-thirties, a year before she died, I paid a visit to my grandmother. As I walked up the sidewalk to her house, she opened her screen door. She stared at me as if she didn't recognize me. When I kissed her cheek, she said, "But you've gotten so beautiful!" The section titled "It's Not about Race" confronts the traumas of being different. Poems of anger and reconciliation, they're my warning that I give good smile but watch out for my teeth.

The last section in this collection, "Gleanings," acknowledges how life comes to us in the small details that remain when the major upheavals subside. Specifically, the poem "Heartlands" refers to the San Joaquín Valley's endless expanses—what Gaston Bachelard called "intimate immensity." When I was a child and a young woman, that immensity ended with the coastal range on one side, the Sierra Nevada foothills on the other. Later, "Heartlands" for me came to refer to the San Diego County landscape, a space scented with sage heavy as wet pillows, a scent so heavy you can touch it. This is what I touch when I write the space I call home.

Acknowledgments

Mil gracias to the book's special godparents: Ray González, Sandra Alcosser, Glover Davis, Marilyn Chin, Toi Derricotte, Cheryl Savageau, Forrest Hamer, and Frances Payne Adler for their support and generous readings of portions of this book. Abrazos and besos to my friends and writers in That Thing with Feathers writing group in San Diego: Mary Williams, Joe Milosch, Glory Foster, Sue Luzzaro, Jane Milligan, Jayne Relaford-Brown, Tamara Johnson, and Severino Reyes. A special thanks to the board of directors and the staff of Cottages at Hedgebrook on Whidbey Island, Washington, for the uninterrupted time to work on these poems. Y bendiciones on the computer pros at Central Connecticut State University and Troy Challenger at CSU Monterey Bay: without them, there would be no book.

An Orchard of Figs in the Fall

Cotton Rows, Cotton Blankets

Sprawled on the back of a flatbed truck
we cradled hoes, our minds parceling rows
of cotton to be chopped by noon. Dawn stuck
in the air. Blackbirds rang the willows.

Ahead, a horse trailer stretched across the road.
Braced by youth and lengths of summer breeze
we didn't give a damn. We'd be late, we joked,
stalled by a pregnant mare draped in sheets.

Later, backs to the sun, bandanas tied
to shade our brows, hands laced with tiny cuts;
later, when the labor contractor
worked us through lunch without water; our dried
tongues cursed that mare in cotton blankets
brought to foal in the outlines of summer.

An Orchard of Figs in the Fall

Somewhere deep in the San Joaquín Valley
a ranch foreman prunes limbs of fig trees
planted prior to World War I. Kadota,
honey-colored fig best eaten dried
like the Calimyrna, but smaller, tougher,
 not as sweet. Enduring.

As a child I walked light in the dried fig season
beneath the pale green glow of a hung-low
canopy, its leaves like many-thumbed hands.
Summer winds picked at figs and dirt clods.
Bend, crawl, bend, pick, infinite insult
 to neck, waist, knees.

Any semblance of shade was destroyed
in the noonday sun. Lunch was a blur
of bean burritos, a dash to the outhouse
at the edge of the field, and a thirst
for water on a floor full of sun-baked
 rock-hard terrones.

Once I ran from a boy on a metal brace
who pitched and rolled as he asked me to play.
I ran from the whispered *Tuvo polio.*
I ran from an orchard of figs in the fall,
the stripped trunks and arthritic fingers,
 a grave of limbs gone wrong.

When You Didn't Have to See to Believe

The monster lived on the road to Merced.
No one knew except me. I kept the secret
all those years, never telling anyone, not
even my parents, not even when we'd
pass his house on our regular Sunday drives.
A summer storm gave away his hideout.
Where else for a brute to hide but
in an empty power plant tight to the railroad?
As lightning flowed, the building came to life.
Windows flashed blue, panes crackled,
orchards heaved their too-ripe fruit.
From the back seat of our car, I listened
to his roar. I knelt on the floorboards,
whispered why Merced, why the center of a valley
so hot in summer you got nosebleeds,
a valley so foggy in winter
you'd lose your hand if you held it in space.
On moonless nights I'd fight to stay awake.
I feared he'd appear in my dreams, steal me.
If I parted my blinds, his face loomed
closer than the boy's next door. I blew
shrill notes through my flute, blared triplets
to cover my gasps. His breath filled my room.

Memorizing the Center of Time

Drops of memory collect,
hold shape long enough to form
a smear across a slide plate.
There's no other spot like this,
no other empty lot whose paths
form an "X" where they bisect
in a hot valley,

a lot littered with beer cans
whose dancing bears promote
El Mejor Sabor—refresh
yourself—and you inhale
the aroma from the cans,
marvel how like the uncles'
aftershave they smell.

Unravel a segment of time
where closed space offers refuge.
A favorite grapevine yields
a cloud of bee dust, its trunk
a perch you share with finch
and sparrow, lives trellised
to an empty lot.

Look at that "X" again,
how precisely lines begin
at each corner, where empty
wax tubes of Kool-Aid puddle
in lime, orange, and grape:
this vine, this lot, this one-block walk
to the candy store.

Squaring the Names

When we caught lice in third grade,
Tony's mother soaked his hair
in kerosene. His hair fell out
exposing a football-shaped skull.
 Pelón, we chanted, *Pelón,*
 cabeza de melón.

We forgot his name
but not his bald head, not
even when his hair grew back.

The Chávez's oldest girl
wore a cheerleader's skirt
and a letter on her boxy
orange sweater.

La Barbie, we called her,
as in Barbie Doll, and Jorge
was her football captain Ken.

And there was Pineapple
for his chunky shape, Shorty
because he was, and Be-Tween
the youngest of the twins.
My favorites were Punkin
with her fiery-red hair
and Hollywood for his gold chains.
For awhile I was the barrio
sweetheart, la consentida,
with my Shirley Temple curls
to my waist. Too bad I wore bifocals.
 Bookworm. Brain.
 Coke-bottle eyes.

My aunts switched to Spanish
when I came around. I stayed

bilingual. When they caught me
listening to the gossip about
my godmother, her boyfriend
ten years younger, they shrieked:
      ¡Coliche! ¿Quién te invitó?

I told an uncle that he lacked
the right chromosome
which was why he only had
daughters. I'd read that somewhere.

I'll never forget how my mother
signaled with her eyes,
warning, yet amused,
how my uncle hollered,
      *¡Cabrona! Somebody should wash
      your mouth out with soap!*

All these names I saved for myself.
When my mother introduced me
to her uncle last year, she said:
      *Soy Tomasa, esposa de Manuel,
      y ésta es mi hija, Diana,
      la más grande.*

There it was, the formal genealogy:
      *I am Tomasa, wife of Manuel,
      and this is my daughter, Diana,
      the oldest.*

I am Diana la cazadora
keening calls to the hunt
on moon-hard nights.
I respond to orejona,
ears bent to the shape of your sighs.
Call me la chismosa,
your secrets glide in neon past my gaze.

Charm me with cabrona,
rutting female goat,
name of admiration
for those who won't back down.
Beware la hocicona,
the unmuzzled jaw,
the one whose heart rules her tongue,
the one whose tongue savors life.

La Curandera

She shuffles to the door on faded scuffs.
Her breasts sway beneath the bodice of her muumuu
and the hands that welcome me are warm,
the skin like old paper crumpled then smoothed.
She is la curandera, faith healer, my nana.
We face each other, child to grandmother,
the trusting balance of young to old.
Mija, did you give it to the priest,
did he bless it? she asks. She takes the emblem
of the brown-skinned Virgin from my palm.
The sun is in her face, her eyes water.
Some say she can read minds. She makes us drink
infusions of gordo lobo, fat wolf,
when we are sick with fever from the flu.
She prescribes a tea of estrella de anís
to calm the itching rash of measles; a tea
of manzanilla for those who can't sleep.
The new Irish priest didn't understand.
Witchcraft, he snorted, and refused to bless
the scapular. So at Mass I placed the badge
with its rubbed smooth image in my prayer book
hoping to catch stray blessings. *Kyrie eleison.*
Tonight the old women of the neighborhood
begin a novena, nine days of prayer
for a dying man. Doña Juanita attends,
her black lace shawl clipped to her bun.
Her husband lies on their bed at home, swaddled
with sheets fresh from the line. The women fan
their black damask skirts on red Windsor chairs.
Nana displays the scapular. Hail Marys rise.
I can never go to heaven if the old man dies.

La Llorona

Cuca bellies down, her scarred arms from last year's fire
laced in silky dirt. The chinaberry rustles; Cuca begins—

> *When she comes, she comes*
> *in a long, white skirt*
> *all wet and dripping*
> *from where she drowned*
> *her babies in the river.*

We shiver; goosebumps dot our legs. Cuca pauses for effect,
her voice hushed. We listen to her nails scratch her arms,
try not to look at the dried dark scabs coated with dust.

> *Huuy,* she calls,
> *¿dónde están mis hijos?*—

Where are my children? Cuca stares at me—

> *She can hear her children call her.*
> *She peeks through bedroom windows,*
> *looks for kids who sleep alone,*
> *the ones who cry out in their sleep.*

Cuca knows I sleep alone, but I avoid her eyes. Instead, I catch
on the tale of a mother who drowns her children when their father
leaves for a younger, richer woman, like my uncle who left my aunt
for the egg rancher's widow. Cuca tenses; her fingers claw the air—

> *You can't hide, she can go*
> *through anything. If you cry,*
> *she will offer you pan dulce*
> *pa'que se te quita el susto,*
> *then steal you away.*

My youngest brother bolts. Too late, we tear after him,
dreading our mother's anger as he begs her not to drown him,
as he tells her why he cries.

That night I dream La Llorona, hair caked with mud and tule rush,
lifts me, plants me, bulb of iris in my mother's garden,
bubble of head inches below water.

The Creek That Bears the Salmon

Once upon a time
the creek prowled my town
bearing sleek salmon
making for the coast.

It tore tomatoes
from Bandini's field,
hung heron feathers
in the tule marsh,
tangled roots of eucalyptus
at its banks.

Its trill threaded trains
along the Santa Fe tracks;
its piping lured bombers
from storms farther north;
its hum hustled rigs
hauling wrist-thick carrots,
tomatoes so ripe
their scent stained the air.

So when the creek sighed my name
below the G Street bridge,
carved the shape of my smile
on mud-slick slopes,
I broke for the coast
with the salmon.
When your time comes
to navigate the valley,
listen to the creek:
it keeps perfect time.

La Madrugada

The radio alarm clock sputters.
A liquid-lipped announcer cries,
  K-X-A-X, Radio Campesino.
I pull the covers higher
but can't escape the call:
  Es la hora de amanecer,
  aquí viene la madrugada.
Here it comes,
this day's dawn.
Once again I hear the strains
of strung-tight violins,
the flutes' galloping trills,
opening to an old standard,
"La espiga,"
the eager wheat ear
ripening for love.
Soon I'll brave
my leche con café.
I'll clutch my favorite bowl,
cringe as the soft-cooked egg
squirms to my spoon.
I'll marvel at the squirt of yolk,
how it caramelizes fresh white bread.
Then, teeth brushed,
hair pomaded into braids,
I'll grip the wire handle of my lard can,
rush to claim a window
to the predawn air.
Knees pop, hips and back
spasm, but it has never
been better or worse
than this: the way sunlight slips
overhead, the plopping sound
as figs fill my can,
the sweet-salt toil
of harvesting the fields.

When Living Was a Labor Camp Called Montgomery

When living was a labor camp called Montgomery

you joined the family each summer to sort dried figs.
From Santa María to Gilroy, Brawley to Stockton, you settled
in rows of red cabins hidden behind the orchards.

You recall how the red cabin stain came off on your fingers,
a stain you pressed to your cheeks so you looked like
Dolores del Río, the famous Mexican actress.

Her high-sculpted glow stunned the boys who dogged you
to the theater, the coolest building in town, where you forgot
the San Joaquín heat and fruit flies.

You wiggled on velvet-backed chairs, split popcorn with
your cousins. When the film's hero, the rancher's son, rode
horseback to the river and spied Dolores washing her hair,

you'd swoon. Just for a moment, a small eternity, the hero's
hacienda, its dark wood beams and low-slung chandelier, were yours.
You were tall and thin and everything looked good on you.

To tell the truth, though, you preferred Lauren Bacall's whistle.
So at the packing shed you eyed your brothers' friends, not
the pickers, the carpenters, those who wanted out

of the fields. You picked one with a full-mouthed smile, not
your mother's choice but a tall man with papers who wanted
to join the army and live in L.A.

And perhaps, in the end, everything didn't look good on you.
Maybe your hair didn't look good dyed auburn; maybe
pillow-breasted women weren't meant to wear sheaths.

You visit the camp each summer reunion. Your sisters snatch
peeks at your husband. His teeth still look good. A cousin
glides you through a cumbia; you dreamt he kissed you once.

You catch the stench of rotting figs, of too-full outhouses.
The nose closes off. You feel how hot it was to sleep, two
to a mattress, the only other room a kitchen.

You thought your arms thickened long ago lugging trays of figs.
You thought you had peasant ankles. You thought you could die
in the camp and no one would know your smell.

Tísica
(Ahwanee Tuberculosis Sanatorium, Yosemite Valley, 1958)

What can your dusty shack
in a San Joaquín labor camp
say to this converted cavalry barracks
nestled below Yosemite's Half Dome,

this tuberculosis sanatorium
downwind from Tuolomne Meadows
and the Ahwanee Hotel,
elegant lodge for wealthy tourists.

What you cleaned from the walls
of your shack stayed with you,
the stuff of last year's tenants,
their dried and caked remains:

uncooked beans, spilled rice,
the shells of roaches plastering
the cracked ceiling and floor.
The browned, yellowed stains

on the mattress troubled you
but sweat and blood betray
a life picking fruit, you thought.
You thought your cough reflected

dank air—mist rising from the creek;
bad air—the outhouse midday.
But your skin sallowed, the bags
beneath your eyes deepened.

Consumed by cough and sweat, you wait
as veiled nuns collect your ochered sheets
each daybreak. You approve.
Removed from friends and family

allowed no contact, you bask invisible
in a fine air of pine and wealth,
numbed isolation in a nation's preserve.
You flatten clay, form rows of Half Dome

ash trays, spoon holders, coded messages
urging release. If air alone could rise, sift,
dissipate tuberculosis passed
among migrant families, you might have fled

this sanatorium months ago. Instead, you stall
with patients labeled unclean, unclean, sinful.
You hear the whispered tísica, tubercular,
nightmare of the poor, the dread disease.

Repatriation

they called the process. Red wheat senators
and corn belt congressmen, Oklahoma farmers
and stock market analysts bellowed,
Repatriation, a long word dipping
into cracks and crevices, an abstract word,
no conscience here, a shorthand way to say

> *Get them out, we're in a depression,*
> *they don't speak our language,*
> *send them back to where they come from,*
> *they're taking our jobs in the fields.*

A heartbeat later, a bright-lit nation cleansed you,
sped you away to Zacatecas, to Guanajuato,
the border's membrane just a breath away.
On the other side, L.A.'s finest clashed
with dust bowl migrants, native sons chasing
a wind-blown land. A nation's troubadour
hummed *This land is your land, this land is my land,*
a distorted credo in either tongue.

Operation Wetback, 1953

The day begins like any other day.
Your daughter soaks a second diaper,
chortles as she shoves her soft-cooked egg
to the floor. Knees pressed to cracked linoleum,

you barely notice as your husband strokes
your belly. *Mijo,* he croons, prophetic plea,
then squeezes your nalgas as if to gauge
for ripeness. As he edges past, you notice

how his blue shirt blurs against the summer sky,
how sky absorbs his patch of blue, then empties.
Moments later, a truck groans, moves on,
carting rumblings of men headed for the fields.

Years later, you tell your son and daughter
of that anguished day, how green card migrants
vanished from the camps. You tell your children
how news gripped the camps of trains headed south

loaded with wetbacks. You never tell your children
what you can't forget: how you failed to squeeze back,
failed to wave good-bye, failed to taunt him
with viejo sinvergüenza. You never tell your children

how you forget this one man's voice—a voice
that brushed your ears, your hair, a path down your back—
a voice that blends with sounds of a truck
that never brought him home.

Softball and Tomato Fields

They swarm like ants from the edge of the field,
la migra, the brown horde of them. They take
the best away: Manuel, the meanest pitcher

in the league; Frankie, who could have played
for the Brooklyn Dodgers; Monchie, too busy
looking at the clouds to catch a pop-up fly.

They take the best from Texas and Sinaloa,
from Arizona and Nuevo León—
dutiful sons, faithful husbands swept up

in the net. No matter if they're legal,
no matter if they have papers, in this game,
runners caught between bases are all picked off.

She Tends Bar

while she waits for a man
she hopes will make his way
north, slip across the border
from wherever the trains
derailed him. She tends bar
while she waits on a man
who slides a tip across the counter,
a man who studies her
as she wipes beer and sweat
from the counter, who spies
as she tucks his tip
next to a baby's teething ring.

She hurries a tray of beer
to a table wreathed in smoke.
Two men lean back, tracing
the curve of her hips, their eyes
working the rise of her skirt.

In the way some men bet the dogs,
others the cockfights,
others that the moon holds rain
to spoil next week's work,
the man pomaded with Dixie Peach
bets odds tonight he'll cup
the front of the barmaid's blouse.

The woman who tends bar
bites her tongue as she walks away,
feeling dangerous towards this man
who earlier offered to walk her home,
who swore it would be a privilege
to change her ceiling bulb
and unstop her sink besides.

El Porvenir

he paints on the front of his store—
    for the time to come—
for women who enter singly,
bare-legged, sandal-footed
through a screened wooden door
hung on metal springs
so that each open/close
yields another scent to savor,
another scent his wife cannot remove.

He paints stucco walls a peach to draw
the sun's attention, to draw the eyes
of women to fresh-killed goats, whole
and dead-eyed, laid out in his case.

He installs deep wood bins for piles
of bleached hojas, cream-colored sheaves
ridged on one side, smooth on the other,
bins that darken from the sweat of hands
drawn to the best leaves.

He keeps the floors bare to capture
footsteps. His eyes keep score
of the day's parade, women scooping
black and pinto beans. He charts
the daily harvest at the scales,
the sacks of beans, rice, onions.
El sinvergüenza, the women snicker,
when he croons a taste for one's
steaming beans, another's green corn tamales,
a third's spicy pollo en mole,
this man who savors the musk
of women straight from the fields.

Turns at the Dance

The man who loves rancheras holds out his hand
gently, formally, again and again,
bends to the sound of each woman's voice.
The pattern of rejection makes him stiff.
Soy de Michoacán, he says, plaid shirt crisp
with starch, string tie taut around his neck.
The woman in the rose-patterned skirt rises
to his hand. She giggles when he twirls her
to a spin. His hand catches on her back.
She wonders for a moment if her hair
would snag at his caress. When she stumbles
on the beat, he takes her by the elbow.
She wonders if she'd flinch if he lightly brushed
her cheek. He wonders if a time might come
when he could study how her eyes are flecked
with gold, watch beads of sweat collect
along her forehead. Could there come a time
when he would ask *¿Dormiste bien?* and
¿Cómo te sientes? over morning coffee?
She steadies on her too-high heels, pretends
he doesn't follow when the music ends.
She weighs his invitation to the dance.

Green Corn Season

You promised you would never keep secrets from me.
You told me everything: how rain tinkled on your bedroom walls;
how you thought you were dying the first time blood spotted
your panties; how your stomach lurched when the boy you liked
asked you to the prom. When you came home that night,
all you said was that you danced in a field of green corn,
dirt smell old beneath your feet, your moonlit steps
as the tape rang out *Rosamaría fue a la playa* and you said
you hoped one day you'd swim at the beach.

Now you're pregnant almost three months, but
you haven't said a word. A mother notes these things
about her daughter: the way tipped breasts swell
like egg whites whipped twice their volume, no more
small whorl of nipple brought to peak; your hunger
for ice cream on ripe melon, how you spoon small bites
as if to guide them to specific cells.

I bear full responsibility. You were my grand design,
part nature child, part small philosopher propped
in a blind of apricot, a favorite book crooked
in the "V" of a branch. Often I watched you set aside
your book to study light playing on slim, tanned thigh,
the play of skin against leaf and bark, all part
of the same glowing world. I watched you grow lush,
tender, pulling for the sun.

Some things a daughter needn't tell her mother:
how we wax gibbous on beds of disked fields,
moonlight glancing off sloped shoulders; how we swoon
in the earth's perfume, consumed by an urge
to begin in the green corn season.

Serpentine Voices

Serpentine Voices
FROM SILENCE

How many voices can I plum in this poem.
Tricky poem, sometimes in the first person "I,"
as in sometimes the story is mine,
as in me the author,
the first-person narrator,
and at times the voice becomes
third person "we,"
plural, not imperial,
because sometimes
we were all voice, girlfriends,
mis amigas, de parte de,
on behalf of all of us,
voices drowning out
that choking silencio,
that pestilent marshland of a vacío.
Because we were something.
God, we were something else.

HUELGA

Fresno slumps late summer.
Raisin grapes dry on paper trays.
Crepe myrtle, purple plum burnish
the college campus, student body twice
the size of my hometown.
Winemaking meets
a general education mode.
Professors serve finals
at the Gallo winery.
Agriculture majors milk cows
at dawn, saunter back to plates
of thick bacon, butter-basted eggs.
Some become lawyers; others
shoulder family farms;
still others sell the family farms
to local speculators.
We never knew their names
but sun red and neckish,
their faces grimace
from across the barricades
as we chant
¡Huelga! ¡Huelga! ¡Huelga!

THE FARMWORKERS' DAUGHTERS

Khaki, everywhere khaki.
Not us, boy.
Our dads wear khaki
in the fields, khaki
cruddy with suck plums
and peaches, khaki topped
with white dress shirts pressed
by mouthy daughters
who iron their hair
so it lies like banners
over shoulders,
daughters who swear
to wear miniskirts
and tight, tight dresses
when we're outta sight.
We'll be so outta sight.

Emiliano Zapata Eyes

Laura's so goofy over him,
his Emiliano Zapata moustache
and burning eyes, the raven waves
of his hair. All he needs is a horse,
a hat, and he could be poster boy
for the movement: Campus Crusader.
Campus Crusader at the microphone
crooning fight songs to the masses
severe body taut beneath poncho
and requisite khakis.
Exquisite.
¡Qué tonta!
As if he cares.

Campus Crusader took lunch
with the college president.
They scrutinized the weather.
(Will the rain hold?
Do raisins mold in the rain?)
Then Campus Crusader promised
we'd vacate the library.
He may have promised names.

Somebody should tell Laura
his wife in Sanger fled Durango
when she was 17.
She packs tomatoes,
packs his parents to the doctor,
packs their son to day care.
She sends him care packages
when he's too broke to eat.
Somebody should tell Laura
about the WASP girlfriend

in his apartment complex,
a real wasp, you know,
wasp-thin waist
in a hive of drones.

The Love Affairs

As if short skirts make a bad
reputation. Nalgas, heck yes,
you can see my nalgas,
full curves beneath a white summer dress,
the only way I'll wear white again.
You who always liked my ass,
who swore you'd always take care
of me. You with your preacher talk,
so respectful to my parents, *¿Mande Ud.?*
whenever they asked you a question.
If I'd known you'd go back to her
I never would have opened my door to you,
never would have slipped beneath the sheets
so scared you wouldn't like me,
so scared you'd tire of a nervous virgin.
I may as well give it to anybody.
Lárgate de aquí. I never want
to see you again, and you tell me
she's pregnant.

THE GIRLFRIENDS

Rosie/I
got pregnant.
Her/my
lover swore it wasn't
his/their
fault. It was
cinco de mayo/
16 de septiembre
and I/we/she/he/they
broke loose.
Loose hips whipping
through cumbias,
ankling through rancheras,
hips grinding
through night-long sets
of lovemaking, the intensity
of a rolling tent revival.
Rosie/I had a
miscarriage/baby.
Rosie/I thought
I/she
was lucky.

The Old Married Couple

He never told anyone he couldn't swim.
I didn't know he couldn't swim.
We tripped.
My Yoko Ono to his Dylan Thomas.
We played "Knights in White Satin"
at dawn, steamed brown rice,
sautéed onions for dinner.

I loved his body,
a small-muscled body.
Each knot and ripple etched
his skin, bronzed
like our son's first shoes.
He called me lush,
his hands sweeping low,
slow, Morse coding
closer to the goal.

Our goal. He would publish
a first book of poems by 25;
I'd teach art at a local college.
I reached my goal.

I didn't go to the lake
but I see him at night
behind my eyelids,
water toying with his chin,
lips, eyelashes.
No one notices.
No one hears his shouts:
I'm drowning, I can't swim,
this big joke, this grown man
who never left the fields
long enough to learn to swim.

My husband who knew
the verb to live
deserved to live.

¿Que viva la raza de bronce?
Yes, I live,
he did live,
we should have lived.

The Hearings

We weren't unaware, stuck here
in this death bowl of a valley.
There were just more pressing matters.
We knew about the moratorium.
We had brothers in Vietnam.
We knew the death counts
newscasters never mentioned.
Just give them a live feed
and let them sail away.
Hey, they / we
didn't want to know the truth
Our concerns were more immediate,
we argued.

Remember the hunger hearings?
We were there.
Taking shorthand in English
and in Spanish,
transcribing notes all night.
We fought for food stamps,
not those god-awful commodities,
weevils in the rice,
beans so dry a week's soak
couldn't get them back to plump.

We fought for food stamps
as if books of coupons
could ease our mothers' hearts,
as if coupons could fight
fungus in a brother's boots,
could fight letters filled
with silence in the night.
We fought for food stamps

while our mothers prayed
to the bleeding heart of Jesus
enshrined above the TV,
desperate pleas through channels
to bring the sons home safe.

El Movimiento

Hey, ése, you heard about that righteous
lawyer down in L.A., a real carnal, man.
You know, he got the people off who marched
on that church on the white side of town.
Man, he's got so many rucas, all of them
young enough to be his daughters. ¡Pura madre!
He's got a book out, you know, calls himself
a buffalo. Yeah, and he wants to write a book
about el movimiento, something about cockroaches.

METAPHORIC COCKROACHES

Experts theorize cockroaches survive anything.
Give them a nuclear explosion, they come back
stronger than ever. I think this means you can step
on us a million times but we'll come back in droves.
I despise cockroaches. I've tossed out my share
of roach motels; I know where they end. Better
a roach at the end of a clip any day. Anyway,
cockroaches come apart in the city. All that stress.
Out here in the country, anyone can be a roach.
For myself, raisin grape makes better metaphor.
Burnt brown, juicy, enough folds and wrinkles to offer surprises
the rest of one's life. A treat. Sweet. Iron-rich. Sustaining.

CODA: LEVÁNTATE, NO PIDAS MÁS PERDÓN. . . .

A dry hot wind zings through my pores.
I ponder the fate of betrayed loves,
extinct buffalo. I strain to hear the end
to old songs, landscaped lives; the river
of voices never leaves. Chilled beef tongue lies
cradled in crystal, the delicate flavor enhanced
by fresh garlic and tomatillos. I created this dish
for myself. I listen to Los Lobos by myself,
pour myself a tall glass of beer.
Women live longer than many men—
so the actuarial tables say. At the end,
I'll be better off with my tongue married
to a sauce simmered long after buffalo
disappeared from the plains.

What the Curandera Knows

With a candle and a canning jar
she draws the fever from measles
and the evil eye. No rings, no lipstick,
no smile, she flames the bottom of the jar
until smoke whorls inside.
The hairs below her long black sleeves
are singed. She whips the mouth
against my chest so the skin beneath
deadens, blisters. Behind my eyes
I see the candle in her hand,
myself before it, how I go
on, off, on, off
like the round red eye
above the confessional,
a light that marked the sins
I didn't tell the priest,
the way a lover touched my breasts,
the fold behind my knees,
or somewhere deeper.
The curandera interrupts me with
¿Y qué querías saber?
What do I want to know?
What do I ask?
I eat, dance, love, yet cry,
¿Pero qué más hay?—
What more is there?

Turning Trays

Each vineyard is a world of crosses.
They sink in fog each winter, in summer
dangle green redemption. Late August,
grapes sugar even as you cut. You must cut
and lay and spread and turn each tray
again and again. Flesh shrivels,
browns in the sun. Bronzed nuggets
fall from the stem, and you,
as far from the beginning as the end,
cannot walk away.
You cannot escape turning trays.
One row ends; another begins.
You must finish this row
and the next
and the next.

I once feared I'd end up stuck mid-row,
a line of brown paper trays behind me,
neat bunches of grapes splayed across
each tray. Raisin grapes trailed me,
pearls the size of my fingertips.
Here is where I tackled imagery:
taut flesh between my teeth,
sweet liquid down my throat.
Here is where I struggled for the end
of each line, no dirt roads or dry canals
to turn me back. I learned to savor
strands of words, weigh their ripe perfection.
I learned to measure a scrub jay's call,
a dragonfly's rainbow flight.
I learned there is no stepping away,
no leaving behind what remains:
one more row to turn,
unfinished lines to tend.

Breasting the Rogue

Valley Fever

I was a favorite niece, the only daughter
and no virgin: the valley grew too small.
So I pawned my first flute and typewriter
and headed for a place that had it all—
classy subtitled films, canyon-laced coast,
flamed leaves to the east and desert beyond.
But meadowlarks flashed yellow today. Lost
for a time where fog-inspired dreams abound,
the uncle who swore by San Francisco
moved back home. These days I yearn for flat lands
ridged with tule marsh, my old grammar school
now an earthquake hazard. I trace my hands
down the lines of my mother's family tree:
fifth down on the left, my branch grows slowly.

Other Marías

Once there were 50 Marías
each with 50 lovers. There was
María Luz the secretary
who crooned Latin-French-Spanish to
her Brazilian sailor, the son
of a diplomat who brought her
music boxes from Las Vegas
where he slept with María del Pilar
who lay with the finish carpenter
who stroked her calves
as if to raise the grain on a
staircase finial. María de los Dolores
caught a lash from the bricklayer
whose dust raised welts on her shoulders
while María Elena fixed paella
for the Spaniard who sneered
at her Yanqui taste for sweet beef and lettuce,
always lettuce with every meal.
María de las Rosas snuck
Marxist tracts into the copy
room for her Tijuana lover
who multiplied them hundredfold
so he could pass them to his morenita,
María la Negra from Cuba who scored
on a Venceremos Brigade with
the insurance sales boyfriend of
María de Jesús (mother
of a two-year-old) who, awaiting
trial on drug-smuggling charges caught
her lawyer's eye which provoked his
mother, María de los
Remedios, who refused to bless
their union saying her son who
would make a fine judge should marry
a pure María, undefiled,

not this María with child
who favored the creak and sproing of
cheap motel beds, the smoke-wine scent
of pliant sons who matched
her rising rhythm, not
this passionate María,
definitely not a virgin.

Occupant: Blue Roof Apartments

The mail addressed to Occupant
wants to bury me cheap,
wants to sell me a family album
or *Funk and Wagnall's Encyclopedia*
on the installment plan.
Not one letter offers what I want
or need: a set of retread tires,
a gold crown for that top left molar,
that 49ers jacket my son saw at the mall.
Their surveys don't show
that plopped beneath
our blue-roofed apartments
we are all on welfare
or navy enlistees.
Our cobalt blue roofs flash
　　Here we are,
　　the anonymous poor
a sea of misery stored
in the city's largest housing complex.
The apartments next door
with understated brown roofs,
security guard and pool
is where we'll move
when we get the next job,
the next raise,
the next big promotion,
that next step up
that guarantees us mail
addressed to us by name.

Pressing Realities

Scent of pine enters my window
joins with the scent of sinsemilla
shimmering in the breeze.
From my stereo Miles squeezes
past "Sketches of Spain."
Flute to my lips
past forgotten
future dim
I could be in a cabin
on the shores of Bass Lake
or haloed in a lightning storm
in the hollow of Tuolomne Meadows.
Instead, from across the way
my neighbor interrupts:
    Loca, are you smoking
    that shit again?
In a complex where everyone
knows your business, reality
always intrudes. Laura,
who hates to work
    —*It's too demeaning*—
borrows five bucks till Friday
every Friday.
Little Eddie climbs the spindly pine
outside my bedroom window;
he never knows what he might see.
Big Eddie hooks up my stereo
then volunteers to unhook my bra.
Subsidized, on the poverty line,
reality might undo me.

Quality Poor

You can't be poor to live in the blue roofs.
Only quality low-income here, the top 10%
of the poor, a pink-collar ghetto
of important titles: the account executive
who picks up her boss's son's birthday cake
during her lunch hour and hopes he'll settle
his bill; the hospital's bilingual stenographer
who can't afford her medical benefit premiums;
the executive assistant at the welfare office
who qualifies for food stamps to make ends meet.

Management, that's what we want.
We all want to manage here: balanced
checkbooks with a little extra
at the end of the month; balanced
lives that don't catch us scrubbing
toilets at 2 A.M.; balanced 3.5 kids
who never tear the window screens.
Instead we endure, reduced to being
managed because we stand in line for aid.

Raisins in Summer

Friday before payday we haul the kids
to one apartment, feed them homemade
flour tortillas, 50 at a crack, a huge pot
of beans, another of rice, then order
them out the door with a round of
    Don't climb the trees
    you'll break your necks.
    Watch your little sister / brother.
    I better not catch you
    sticking rocks in your ears /
    pouring sand down the slide.
Then we kick back at the Formica table:
Yolanda, a San Antonio transplant
whose husband left her, pregnant
with their third child, for anything blonde
or redheaded, nothing brunette;
la Josie, who taped her husband's
you-know-what while he slept
after she heard the sax lessons
he was giving to the neighbor
and he only played clarinet; and Sonia,
whose mother watched Sonja Henie
in black and white, only our friend Sonia
usually wore her black with greenish purple
above her eye or on her cheek and once
on her left breast. We push back
the tablecloth, then kill a half gallon
of cheap burgundy. That's what you do
on Friday nights, too broke to go out,
asses stuck to cheap vinyl seats. We paint
our toenails Raisins in Summer and joke
about the date who met our kids, then vanished.

Next Friday, payday, after the bills go out;
after we hear the latest from our kids' fathers

on why their checks are late; after we treat
the kids to a splash at the beach, hot dogs
over a fire ring; we'll cruise the aisles
at the local market, stock up on boxes
of macaroni and cheese, hamburger
and tuna helpers. We'll freeze family packs
of ground beef textured with gristle,
stack cans of the cheapest tuna in rows
of three. We'll replenish the bins
with a sack of potatoes, another of beans,
and hope we don't get mealy moths before
we finish the rice. Once again we'll shelve
who we once were, who we might
have been, alongside our unmet desires.

The Clog of Her Body

Breathe in, blow out, legs in stirrups, bottom up,
eyes glued to a happy face tacked to the ceiling.
Next to it a smiling Burt Reynolds asks
Did you check your breasts today?
Each time the doctor presses, you grit,
grin, clutch the nurse's hand.

You had a hard, big body like the mahogany bowfront
that held your family's china. Your boyfriend said
he liked your legs—a fawn's legs tapering
to a narrow instep. Your mother warned
Keep your panties on, mija. I won't be responsible
if you take your panties off.

That first time you got pregnant, stretch marks silvered
from your crotch to your ombligo, shone with lotion
that made your panties look like parchment.
For Easter Mass you squeezed into a blue and white
striped minidress, slipped into your red leather heels.

When you left the church that day, a middle-aged man
in a gray Oldsmobile—fins snaking down the street—
pulled alongside and offered you a ride.
It was Charlie Cruz, Nadine's dad, the one who looked
so sexy at your high school graduation.

Remember how he looked you over like a box
of nuts and chews, your belly out to there, your hair
pulled back with a tortoise-shell barrette. You said,
No thank you. He said, *What if we just took a ride somewhere?*

And you said, *Muy agradable, Mr. Cruz.*
I could use a bathroom. By the way,
excuse me while I pass some gas.
I don't get morning sickness, just this gas.

You could have called his wife,
said how you saw Charlie down on Sixth today,
how fine he looked in his best silk tie and asked
could she stop giving him liverwurst for lunch.

When you had your daughter, the boss pressed
against you in the copy room. White flakes dusted
his pink forehead and peach-scented hair. Andy was
a brilliant man, four degrees and no profession,
supervisor at the welfare intake office.

When he accidentally touched your milk-hard breasts,
told you they were the largest sweat glands
on the human body, you thought of offering him
a peek, unsnapping your shirt, removing the now-soaked
yellowed nursing pad that reeked of soured cream.

When you got home, Ronnie rubbed the spot
in the middle of your back, the ridges on your shoulders
where your bra straps dug too tight. Those were the nights
your breasts leaked if you slept on your side
or on your back, never mind your stomach.

When Ronnie ran his hand up your thigh,
kneaded for awhile the softest part, then moved
toward the fold, you cried, *No, my stitches.*
He wished that you had murmured,
Ven acá, mijo, what a fine big boy you are.

So when your doctor says it's all worn out
and you need a hysterectomy, listen to his hum
as he spreads you wide. Note his rising heat,
his lust for meat, as he marvels at your moist
pink walls. And when he clips you with his speculum,
don't be shy. Stick your cervix out to there
before you spur him in his sides.

Posteriors for Posterity

How to talk politely
in mixed company
about the behind
the backside part
of the front you can see
the back drop hidden
from your view
except for those
treacherous times
when you lean
way over
then back
over your shoulder
full light against the dark
and a mirror catches
your flanks.

Imagine, strolling
down the street
self-conscious, so
conscious of your jeans
too tight across
your butt
clutching the curve
below the rise
dipping just enough
those matched
rounded onions unless
you're one of those flat
wonders of whom others
mutter *pero ni tiene nalgas*
as if life's success revolves
around a fat, not flat, ass.

Then you shake by
in a sultry mode

and someone shouts
mueve la cintura
and it's not
your waist they desire
but those sweet notes
side by side, crooning
as they dispense
papal blessings.
Then I tell you
that's some ass
that man has
a nice juicy butt.

Breasting the Rogue

We reach a town of barefoot kids. No one
in the car, not my girlfriend, not our sons,
whispers what we think: how poor

they look, dirt sidewalk dusting
skinny feet, a grimy hot sifting
through strands of hair. Here's a town

anchored to the local bar, a town
bare of lawns and potted geraniums,
a town where weedy kids, weedier than our two,

flourish. Odds were we'd end up living in a town
like this, single mothers on welfare, edged
off the map. Instead, college-degreed,

favored we take note of the waitress
we might have been who tells us nothing
but low-down scuzz balls stalk the counter.

On the outskirts of town past a stone bridge
the Rogue winds west. We pull aside.
Picnic time. A pale bluff rises

above a rocky slice of beach.
Good mothers, both of us, we down
bottles of beer while the boys fuss

at raspberry jam and sliced cheese
sandwiches, a feast if you're not
too choosy. These boys are.

Midafternoon, low on food and good humor,
any entertainment makes sense.
They tell us they're going for a swim.

The Rogue narrows in August, maybe
fifty yards. I swear it's the beer, the thick
light pivoting from stands of fir.

I swear they jump right in,
a pair of brown-skinned boys breasting
the Rogue, small rafts in distress.

I can't swim a pool without collapsing;
my friend can't swim at all. Too late,
I voice warnings: cramps, white water,

midchannel crises. I calculate: they've earned
their junior life guard badges. If they float
fifteen minutes, maybe I can save them.

Maybe I can drown, too. Water pommels ears,
legs, back. Life surges that way sometimes,
the dip-pull-dip of bodies flailing for a bearing.

Years later my son reassures me, says
he knew to float a bit, paddle when he tired,
let the current work to his advantage.

But the first time he faltered
my friend and I locked glances.
Life rushes swiftly in one-bar towns.

A Matter of Control

Don't be afraid
at night
on the street,
in the daytime
on the beach,
only one other
keeping time
on the beach
with you,
on the street
behind you,
then silence.
When you turn, he
is almost on you,
calf leather slip-ons
step-for-step
with you, so quiet
on their toes. Don't
be afraid
to run, to hide
inside your eyes.
Keep yourself hard
as he stumbles.
Brush your shoulder,
breasts, hips, when he
runs past, runs on
to the next corner,
over a dune, down
to the next wave.
Don't be afraid
when the phone
rings late at night
and a voice smooths
your floral tights
around your ass.

Perhaps it is
the neighbor's son:
catch how his voice
cracks when you say
his name.
Heed the whisper
on the wind
when you are alone
and the moon is full
on the desert.

Study the lines
of the Joshua tree
taut against the sand.
Wear a dress made
of hemp, earrings edged
with feathers.
Invoke the names
of the grandmothers.
Hear their counsel
in the humming rock.
Cry the *peee-ik*
of the nighthawk,
mouth wide,
head thrust forward,
your shadow flung
against the land.

On the First Day She Made Birds

He asked me   if I had a choice
what kind of bird
would I choose to be.
I know what he thought I'd say
since he tries to   end
my sentences half the time
anyway. Something exotic
he thought. He thought
maybe macaw.
That would fit
all loudmouthed
and primary colored
he would think.
(He thinks too much
I always thought.)
But really   at heart
I'm more
don't laugh now
    an L B J
        little brown job
except   except
I'm not the
flit   from
branch
to   branch   type
such a waste
of energy all that
wing flap
and scritch scritch scratch.
Really now
can you see me
seed pod clamped
between my beak
like some landowner,
Havana cigar

clenched
between his teeth?
No   I think   not
I think
green heron.
You ask why?
Personality
mainly.
That hunched look
wings tucked to neck
waiting   waiting
in the sun
on a wide slab of rock
alongside a slow river
like some old man
up from a bad night's dream
where he's seen his coffin
and you say to him
Have a nice day
and he says   *Make me.*
Oh   you want looks
I'll give you
looks:
long olive green feathers
a trace of
iridescence
I could stand
going out   iridescent
chestnut sides and head
a black crown
yes   a crown
something regal
to flash when you get
too close
dark bill   bright
yellow legs
and that creamy streak

down my throat and pecs
good
        not great
but good   pecs
just enough for a quick
hop to the nest.
The best part
no sexual dimorphism
male   female
both alike
endless possibilities.

It's Not about Race

Las Rubias

1.

dear modern women's magazine the ads say you can be a
breck model too but I know that's not true at least not unless
they bleach my skin to white and lighten
up my curls a bit and that's the rub isn't it because they are
curls not folding underneath my chin straight hair but kinky
curls that like to sneak into my ears and another thing those
motherdaughter shampoo ads daughter smiling with
straight ahead blue eyes naturally and mother smiling down
at daughter except my mom and I would have to rouge our
cheeks like heck to pink them that cashmere shade you use
in your ads yours very truly

2.

I dreamt they queened me
for the county fair.
There I stood,
tiara hooked to my head
waving fake nails
to the crowd,
bra straps pinned
to my sweetheart neckline,
bra straps digging
into my shoulders,
my gym coach squeezing
my shoulders, shaking
me awake.
I could run for Indian
princess, not the queen,
she said, too short,
but I knew the score
as she snatched away
the queen instructions:
doeskin looks better
on Mexican skin.

3.

Admittedly I broke with him first: my first boyfriend, the first boy
I ever kissed, serving kisses beneath the pines against the smell
of aftershave and grilled chicken during the annual church dinner.
But to replace me with Laurie's ash blond hair, install her in the
student council office, play kissypoo games with her before my eyes,
her sharp nose more needle-like each day? How could his mother
let him? I bet her mother didn't know how dark his nipples were.

4.

I like that white meat, my brother writes
from his ship in the Mediterranean.
And blond hair, hair down to their ass
and below if you know what I mean.
I know what he means, this
sinvergüenza, this desgraciado,
this no-respecter of me or my mother,
this brother I never answer.

5.

At the mariachi concert, Spanish rising from
all sides, our matched curls black against the
honey-strawberry-platinum sea around us, my best
friend mutters, *I've never seen so many rubias
since the last time we went to the beach.*

6.

About those cellophaned streaks in my hair:
I didn't want to do it. I strayed slightly or completely.
I bench pressed 65 pounds. I found my body again.
My washboarded abs and ripped buttocks called for accents.
So I stripped from selected lengths what made my hair black.
I strutted young again. I reeked bold. I turned white
overnight from some dubious shock.

7.

Around and through her hair, the setting sun backlights her face,
flushes her cheekbones lit from within by bottles of good red wine.
Her blond hair conducts sun and breeze and friends and I crescendo.

I see what others must see, not what she sees when she inspects her
image, the spreading gray that draws a line between youth and age.
I lean into her hair as we nestle together beside the Pacific.

And I recall Linda, the curly blond farmer's daughter, how we played
on the monkey bars the first day of school, how we crouched below
the sky, arms hooked at the elbows and swore we'd always be friends.

8.

Dear my son,
I hoped you would never
feel the sting of being
dark-skinned, your
black waving hair that curls
at the neck, your lips
traced by darker skin
so like mine. But
take heart: we are
the birds of paradise
against a gold-lit world.

Finding a Way

Where did I leave the recording
of my son's laugh at eight?
Where did I stuff the sheet
with finger-painted palm
so small it nestled in my hand?
My son is old enough
to buy me a beer,
to move half a country away,
old enough to say
he loves me
to say he needs me
to say he appreciates me
to say I'm all he has
when the cops rough him up
for walking the wrong
side of town.

It's Not about Race
   in memory of Yusaf Hawkins

It is thick summer in New York.
No time to be on foot. It's a time
for cars with air conditioning,
for seats covered in cloth or vinyl,
it doesn't matter, just as long
as there aren't any holes.
He hums a snatch of song,
imagines sounds from a car so loud
they make the street *thrum.*
A perfect night, two good friends,
and the prospect of a car
to drive them home.
His friends argue who gets
the front, argue *me, me, I'm first,
no, me.* That's how it is
for a boy with his mother's
lips, hair curled at the forehead;
for a boy with his father's shape
and shoulders like a swimmer,
a good one.

He's dark, too dark for these parts,
this good neighborhood with no
junker cars at the curb, no
trash cans left overnight.
In the sweaty hot people stand
on doorsteps swatting flies,
watch the trio pass, mutter
They got no business here.
The boys don't hear at first
but when they do, it's too late
to avoid the shooting.

A woman held his head in her arms,
memorized his face, crumpled
like a rotting long-stemmed rose.
The hole in his chest closed on its prey.
There was nothing for him to follow,
nothing to anchor him to the newly wet lawn.

These Old Rags

I dig in hard clay dirt,
freesia bulbs scattered
at my knees, pause to admire
rows of landscaped homes,
a scene a friend once called
a soap opera set.
A van pulls up; a voice asks,
¿Habla español?
I'm puzzled by the accent
but respectfully I say
¿Cómo le puedo ayudar?
prepared to direct him past
dead-end streets and canyons.
Do you live around here,
do you need work? he asks.
I rub soil from my hands,
conscious of my work shirt,
my sweat-stained face.
This is my home. I live here.
So clear, so simple.
Yet again, *Do you need work?*
I study his button-down shirt,
knotted tie, propped in a van
HOOVER VACUUMS SALES AND SERVICE
painted on the side. I know him.
His son played on my son's
soccer team. I hesitate,
review my options.
I could pretend I didn't hear,
wait for him to leave.
My grandfather did.
He'd stand, hose in hand,
play a stream of water
on his favorite ash tree,
the trickle speaking volumes.

Or like my dad I could yell
a more satisfying
*Who the hell you think
you're talking to!*
then toss some dirt in the air.
It's my call.
I carefully reply,
*No, but if you need work
I could use a cheap gardener.*

We're All Alike, You Know

My client tells me there's a look,
you know, in the eyes,
the way we talk, you know,
when someone looks at you,
says gypsy, then you're gypsy.
But maybe you're Cuban or
Puerto Rican. I say maybe.
We know. We can tell.
I was in the room next door.
I didn't know this other gypsy
but I knew she was a gypsy.
She asked me to write
her hotel registration card
but I didn't sign. I made her sign
her name. Now they say
the stolen goods,
the useless bonds,
the irredeemable bank drafts
were found in my room.
Not my room. I was in another room.
But we're all alike, you know,
gypsies, liars, cheats, we're all alike.
At the restaurant, I order salad.
My neighbor orders soup.
The waiter brings me soup.
Not mine, I say. I ordered
salad, Caesar salad,
warm garlicky dressing
on romaine leaves.
The soup accuses me
of lying. I look like
the woman who ordered soup.
I am she. Diners stop to listen.
My neighbor confesses

to the soup. Look at us,
I want to say. She's taller,
no glasses, straight hair.
Different. But it's that difference,
right, that makes us all alike?

Gleanings

El Comal: My Grandfather's Griddle

He'd stand outside
watch his garden for hours,
hands behind his back, eyes shaded,
a Panama hat covering
his thick white hair. Indoor air
bothered him.

I never saw him smile
except to salute a grandchild
or slip a quarter in our pockets.
I never heard him talk
except in assent—short,
guttural sounds. I imagined
him playing cards at the tavern,
nodding, speaking only
when asked a question.

It was like that when he gave
the box to my mother. It covered
one end of the kitchen table.
My mother wiped her hands
on the tea towel, looked
at him. She pulled back
when she saw the cast-iron
rectangle, the dimpled handles.
I had never seen my mother cry.

It was all he ever chose
to go inside his home. His wife
furnished it the way she liked.
But he loved pancakes made
with real buttermilk, soggy
with butter and syrup.
With his comal, he made pancakes
for all seven children.

My mother hugged him, tried
to kiss his cheek. He smiled,
embarrassed, grunted *Bueno.*
It was good. There was nothing more to say.

Gleanings

Twilight carves a dimple in the valley.
My dad demonstrates again how best
to glean tomatoes from twice-picked fields.
Vine-ripened, gorged globes scent the air.
Stems prickle skin. I savor the fruit's extra week
in soil. Their heft conjures memory.
In twilight communion, arms green-brown,
Levis stained medieval shades of blue,
our task recalls my father's Arizona,
desert gullied and chaparraled,
his Breughel canvas. I follow his lead,
prepared to accept what's extended:
fruit picked at the end of the day,
landscapes that yield their portion of heart.

Settling

I've never seen his eyes so brilliant, cat's eyes
in a headlamp. They gleamed this way when I was small
before concrete dust induced cataracts and fine red lines.

He wears new pajamas, tan with brown piping.
I have never seen my father in pajamas.
In my memory, he is the shadowy figure
rushing from bed to bathroom
    I'll be out in a minute
a pale figure in white briefs,
all I can see without my glasses.

He shows me blue pajamas; he says he likes them best.
Then he spots a fine brown line in the tan pair. It's hard
not to be impressed by something you can barely see.
    That balloon popped my artery right open.
    Hell, I could have gone like old man Green.
    Remember him? I'd take him tamales
    every Christmas. He sure loved
    your mother's tamales. He died a week
    after he retired, same thing. Boom! That was it.

He wears new cologne, bay rum, fragrant.
Not hospital lemon or evergreen.
He feels . . . good . . . okay . . . still tired.
I have never heard him say he's tired.

These kids don't know how to work anymore.
Almost non sequitur, but I know what he means.
They passed him over for foreman, named the kid
he called Junior, the one he trained for five years.
Plenty of times too sick to work, my dad worked
anyway. What else was there?

One of his prettiest jobs was Tuolomne Meadows,
all those curbs and gutters. Real nice curves—
they're still there, too. That was back in '58.
The parking lots cracked, but that's your blacktop for you.
Anything can sneak between the cracks.

Heartlands

My son hitched a trailer to his Rambler,
packed his surfboard and a freshwater reel,
and moved to Kansas. Why did I expect
we'd stay together when he hooked
his first bass at eight? One June we trolled
rivers from San Diego to Seattle.
He memorized each valley. No doubt
fishing spawned an itch for cutthroat trout.
I thought we'd trace the Pacific Trail;
he dreamed grasslands run with scaled quail.
Our lives together span two decades.
That is how I barely comprehend
a yearning for ponds stocked with catfish,
a passion for wild turkey in the brush.

When Sounds Ring True

Long ago, a woman struck a gong with a hammer made
of the names she called herself when she yelled at her son,
of the names her son yelled back at her
and when the deep groan from the gong was visible
she hung the sound to learn its width and shape,
its bell and butterfly. With her favorite pen
she carefully sliced the sound through its thickness,
watched the sound unfurl, wrap around itself
like a manta struggling to repair a gash.
She listened to it trill, watched it squeeze and grow,
squeeze and grow, until it shook itself apart,
a harmony of oval tones—
like the balance son and mother made years earlier
matching jaws thrust forward to crowd the sky.

Milksnakes and Chocolate Lilies

The children squabbled last night, piercing squall
wrecking my sleep, interrupting a dream about a snake
ribboning past my front door, a childless snake

tasting the trail of a field mouse on my carpet.
Wake up, I shouted, *adolescent hate seeps*
through my floor wax, rising like this snake past curfew.

Wake the man who snores through puerile threats.
Empty the house of mildewed towels.
Order the socks to argyle!

If I could date my discontent, I'd guess Easter.
Alone at home sipping tea, I contemplated
endless bowls of chicken soup for a child's flu.

That moment moved me to climb the Santa Rosa Plateau
because I needed underwire bras,
because I might slip in the mud,

because my cat was dead, my son gone from home,
my husband spotting hawks in Texas.
Past hills of coreopsis, past streams

curried by flood, a pair of chocolate lilies
pressed their advantage. Nodding bell-shapes,
mahogany brown, yielded a sturdy reproof:
life seasoned through drought and flood,
tendrils knifing through thick earth in spring,
bulbs that smolder five dry years then bloom.

If I Trust Myself

This time I swore I wouldn't be
like the squirrels in the park, drop
my guard to the first friendly handout.
I woke before dawn to watch day break
through designer drapes, your own savannah
of stripes, spots, horns, tusks.
I studied how light eased past beige
giraffes and cheetahs, blushed the left side
of your forehead like a large ivory
rose petal lightly veined in blue.
I listened for the way you hacked a bit
when you woke, the way you turned and smiled
when you saw me watching you.
These things take years. At times I broke,
afraid I broke a trust with self, a sense of who I was.
I followed trails to the beach, past sage and Torrey pine.
I picked selected shells at the base of cliffs,
then, pockets filled, I'd find paths back to you,
cleansed, renewed, a gift freely given.
The bond we form insinuates.
I wake these days and smell your scent on me,
the mint that overruns my garden,
a sweet fragrant planting impossible to remove.

He Who Is Like . . .

He toasts me with Cinzano on the rocks.
I sip the sweet liqueur, let it soothe
raw edges. My lips tingle where they meet
the twist of lime, the chilled cut crystal.

A favorite book fills his lap, a yellowed
first edition of *Raintree County,* dust cover
intact. Gently he lifts each page, careful
not to bend the brittled corners.

I'm loyal, he says, soothing me with ruffled
words. I lean my head on his shoulder,
approve my dark hand on his freckled arm.

He slows the turn of yellowed leaves,
reluctant to startle me with an incautious elbow.
I catch his eyes, one hazel, one blue with flecks
of brown. I have never felt a kinder glance.

This Year's Cycle

We lie on the sand, carve tunnels down our sides,
watch them fill with sea. A gust blows water on our thighs,
raises bumps down the length of our spines. Alone, no sons
to embarrass with bared breasts or flab above
our bikinis, we taste salt on our lips, sun on our foreheads.

We dreamt this day forever: no shouts of *What's to eat*
or *Let me up, I can't breathe,* just the two of us,
our own boogie boards, a clean house
when we get home, no cranky kids who don't want to shower.

My son laughs when I tell him I once thought I saw him
standing in the doorway calling *What's for dinner.*
He'd been gone a month. My friend doesn't laugh
when I tell her. She doesn't laugh when I tell her
I've bought a second cat to keep the first one company,
a second set of cries in the night.

These days my friend and I visit sons who hunger
for rolled tacos from Alberto's, not so much for news
from home. Fishing's better, life more languid in Kansas;
music's more sophisticated in New York.

I'll go to Kansas to fish for bluegill and bass. I'll watch
my son clean house, pack lunch, not make his bed.
Thank goodness some things don't change.
We make connections: our sons ask about the beach.

San Diego Aged

My friends and I consume botanas
of whole roasted garlic. Large heads
arrive on steaming platters. We gossip
as we smear cloves on slabs of sour bread.
No men wait for us tonight,
no children stall at a sitter's.
Instead we howl as we recall
a night we ditched boring dates
at a Tijuana hotel, then found
better dates at the best dance floor in town.

I celebrate a birthday with a room
at the Bird Rock Inn, invite
my dearest friends for a night of jazz,
hot chocolate at a nearby pub,
artichoke omelets at Kirby's Café,
a bluff-side view of the ocean.

In May, a friend gifts me roses,
heads bigger than my hands.
Long stems catch their thorns
on the lip of my vase. Their fruit
scents my lips, tickles my throat.

As the harvest moon approaches,
I join one friend for a bonfire
at the beach, another for a concert
by the bay. Consumed by days
that peak perfection, I surround
my life with friends who grow more dear
each day I breathe.

Catalina Eddies

Dusk to dawn, sleek skunks enjoy
avocados in my yard. I give wide berth.
Before the first jogger leaves her prints
on pavement, tough raccoons appear.
They pretend they don't hear my keys click
but they peek to make sure it's me.
Foxes play hide-and-seek,
sometimes on our lawn, other times
across the street, but never after seven;
and brazen squirrels eye me
from the center of the street,
dare me to approach.

Will this be a day for Catalina eddies,
clouds stacked, catching like magnets
in a liquid air swirl?
Or will it blow a fierce Santa Ana,
days of fires in the hills,
smoldering chaparral,
winds so fierce birds do low-crawls?
I cast a spell for Santa Anas
the shallow coast a censer
mixed with black sage, Torrey Pine,
Engelmann oak—precious oils
to fumigate the San Diego skies,
the annual burning pulse.

Runa Pacha

The feeling grows for weeks
before I realize
what has happened.
I got lost in the whir
of concrete and motors
where I hadn't heard a hint
of unaccented Spanish in days,
just guttural clipped tones,
news of lines drawn close,
news of laws to drive
the undocumented south.
An unexpected melody
from a bamboo flute,
a quena tuned to the key
of la, falls into the crack.
My lips curl like a cat's
better to taste the sound
with my teeth. I round
my tongue to say *mucho gusto,*
igualmente, but flaccid muscles
catch on oval tones.
Panicked, I swear to grow
my hair again, let that hank
hang down my back.
I swear to begin each day
with songs sung in softer oooo's,
rolling rrrr's, lilting llll's, rub awake
the parts I've learned to muffle
in this inhospitable air.

This Yearning Season

Another spring done up in blue-eyed grass,
palms studded with orioles, canyons
against premature dawns: who can corner
this yearning season, flyways lapping endlessly?
My garbage disposal's on the blink.
Perhaps this is the year I'll build
a worm farm, red crawlers chubby
as fingers, fattened with mango peel.
The woman who sells me worms suggests
herbal teas, tells me sage survives
Colorado red soil. Six fingers per hand,
she amends raised beds regardless of drought.

On their fiftieth anniversary, my aunt
and uncle renewed their wedding vows. Encased
in white brocade, the bride took
the floor for the opening dance. Violins
curled, horns erupted, guitars plunked.
Baritoned mariachis quavered
   María   bonita-a-a- . . .
Love notes sifted like incense over all.
The groom converged, glasses steamed,
wrinkled from life's ceremony. What to make
of enveloped years as I joined parents,
cousins, everyone my cousin,
spinning in that dim-lit hall?

Transformed by the flickering waltz
younger aunts emerged, high-breasted,
lips unlined, gardenias pinned to marcelled
waves. And men in pleat-stiff pants, hair
ungrayed, honored all their Marías.
Sepia-toned, the scene cobbled memories,
photos snapped in migrant camps decades ago.

Some say seasons never change here; some say
air keeps to sixty in this southwest corner.
But Western and ring-billed gulls endure
a first then second year. Mid-April, impatient
tanagers troll the avocado canopies. Turned loose,
even parrots go feral. Inviolate, I survey
oaks beyond my deck for other lapsed migrants.

The night I spied my first spotted owl,
a friend turned my head with the moons
of Jupiter. One moon sidled by. If a bird,
I couldn't have claimed it for my life list.

But on my life, though no one sang me
a love song, air riffed that wedding night.
Barely visible, air waved like window glass
touched by a vagrant breeze. Aunts, uncles,
mother, father, claim the floor for one
more dance and show me how it's done.

Glossary

Aquí viene la madrugada.	Here comes the sunrise
Barrio	Neighborhood
Botanas	Appetizers
Bueno	Good
Cabeza de melón	Melon-(shaped) head
Cabrona	Hard-headed woman; literally female goat
Campesino	Field-worker
Carnal	Brother; close friend
Cazadora	Huntress; goddess of the hunt
Changuita	Little monkey
Chismosa	Gossip
Coliche	Uninvited guest
Comal	Griddle
¿Cómo le puedo ayudar?	How can I help you?
¿Cómo te sientes?	How do you feel?
Consentida	Favorite
Cumbia	A popular Colombian/Latin-American dance
Curandera	Faith healer; herbalist
De parte de	On behalf of
Desgraciado	Disgraceful one

¿Dónde están mis hijos?	Where are my children?
¿Dormiste bien?	Did you sleep well?
El mejor sabor	The best tasting, most flavorful
Es la hora de amanecer	It's time to get up
Ése	Hey you! (slang); lit. him or that one
Espiga	Wheat ear
Estrella de anís	Anise star
Gordo lobo	Fat wolf, an herb
¿Habla español?	Do you speak Spanish?
Hocicona	Loud-mouthed; lit. big jaw
Hojas	Leaves; in this case, dried corn stalks
Huelga	Strike
Igualmente	Same to you; similarly
Kyrie eleison	Lord have mercy
Lárgate de aquí.	Get out of here
Leche con café	Steaming hot milk with coffee
Levántate, no pidas más perdón.	Get up, don't ask forgiveness
Llorona	Weeping woman
¿Mande Ud.?	You called? At your command
Madrugada	Dawn
Manzanilla	Chamomile
Migra	Border patrol
Mija	My daughter
Mijo	My son
Mis amigas	My girlfriends
Morenita	Dark-skinned woman
Movimiento	Movement; Chicana/o civil rights movement

Mucho gusto	Thank you
Mueve la cintura	Move that waist
Muy agradable	How kind of you
Nalgas	Buttocks
Nana	Grandmother
Novena	Nine days of prayer
Ombligo	Navel
Orejona	Eavesdropper; literally big ears
Pan dulce	Sweet bread; pastry
Pa'que se te quita el susto	To take away the fright
Pelón	Baldy
Pero ni tiene nalgas	But s/he doesn't have a butt
¿Pero qué más hay?	What more is there?
Playa	Beach
Pobrecita	Poor little thing
Pollo en mole	Chicken in thick chile sauce
Porvenir	The time to come; the future
Pura madre	An expletive; similar to motherfucker
¡Qué tonta!	What a fool!
¡Que viva la raza de bronce!	Long live the bronze race!
Quena	Andean bamboo flute
¿Quién te invitó?	Who invited you?
Rancheras	Popular Mexican ballads
Rubias	Blondes
Rucas	Women
Silencio	Silence
Sinsemilla	High-quality marijuana with few, if any, seeds
Soy de Michoacán	I'm from Michoacán

Terrones	Dirt clods
Tísica	Tubercular woman
Tuvo polio	He had polio
Vacío	Void
Ven acá, mijo	Come here, son
Viejo sinvergüenza	Shameless man
¿Y qué querías saber?	And what did you want to know?

Source Acknowledgments

Grateful acknowledgment is given to the following magazines, journals, and anthologies in which some of these poems first appeared:

The Bloomsbury Review "What the Curandera Knows"
El Coro "Tísica" and "The Creek That Bears the Salmon"
Hedgebrook "When living was a labor camp called Montgomery" and "This Yearning Season"
The Helix "Memorizing the Center of Time," "La Madrugada," and "When You Didn't Have to See to Believe"
The Kenyon Review "La Curandera," "When living was a labor camp called Montgomery," "Other Marías," and "Las Rubias"
Magee Park Poets "These Old Rags"
Mid-American Review "An Orchard of Figs in the Fall"
Pa'lante Juntos "The Creek That Bears the Salmon"
Paper Dance: 55 Latino Poets "La Curandera" and "When living was a labor camp called Montgomery"
Ploughshares "Cotton Rows, Cotton Blankets"
13th Moon "Tísica"
Touching the Fire: 15 Poets of Today's Latino Renaissance "Green Corn Season," "Other Marías," "An Orchard of Figs in the Fall," "Turns at the Dance," "Squaring the Names," "La Curandera," "Serpentine Voices," "Tísica," "The Clog of Her Body," and "A Matter of Control"

About the Author

A native of California's San Joaquín Valley, Diana García was born in Camp CPC, a migrant farmworker labor camp owned by the California Packing Corporation. At different times she has been a single mother on welfare, a secretary, a retail electronics store owner, a personnel manager, and a sentencing consultant to criminal defense attorneys. Presently an assistant professor at California State University, Monterey Bay, she coordinates the Institute for Human Communication's Reading, Writing and Critical Thinking Program. She received both her B.A. and M.F.A. at San Diego State University. For four years she was an assistant professor in creative writing at Central Connecticut State University.